sis-te vi-a-tor ‖,sis-te-wé-'ä-,tôr‖ [L] : stop, traveller — used on Roman roadside tombs

for Cathy

COMPLETE TRAVELS

Martin Corless-Smith

WEST HOUSE BOOKS · 2000

Published by
West House Books, 40 Crescent Road
Nether Edge, Sheffield s7 1HN
Distributed in USA by
SPD, 1341 Seventh Street
Berkeley CA 94710

Typeset in 11 on 14 pt Mergenthaler Sabon
at Five Seasons Press, Herefordshire
and printed on Five Seasons
one hundred per cent recycled book paper
by Biddles Ltd, Guildford

ISBN 0 9531509 3 3

The author gratefully acknowledges the following publications: *Chicago Review, Fence, Faucheuse, Interim, Ixion, Explosive, Denver Quarterly, Rhizome, Cello Entry* and *Shearsman*.

'The Garden. A theophany or ECCOHOME' was produced as a chapbook by Spectacular Books.

Amongst the many I would like to thank are Catherine Wagner, Donald Revell, Karen Brennan, Romayne Licudi, Alan Halsey, Ric Caddel, Glenn Storhaug, Joshua Beckman and Katy Lederer. I am grateful to the English Departments at The University of Utah and UNLV for support, especially Utah for the Neff Fellowship and the Steffensen Cannon Fellowship. Thanks always to my parents.

I have taken liberty with some of the works of Sir Philip Sidney, Søren Kierkegaard, Ben Jonson, T. S. Eliot, David Jones, W. S. Graham, Shelley via Alan Halsey, Denton Welch & many others.

Contents

Worcestershire
Mass

I. Nativity

Now Now Nowl Nowl
bec o me ma other
Nor Nor

mothers
poor poor bobtail
poor peewit
the bed prepared
wi' ailanthus chorus childs
a green a vase

I was
we was
were was
born
into December Year
road place

In the market of our
market country cathedra
shown forth by this or that inheritance
defeated gods who think defeat no
may they rest
whosoever will
somewhen
when whencesoever
whenne whensomever
me under
miss
out light
moan green   leight laicht leigcht

li
       fall
ght
       fall
es

lau
       after
ghter
       eve
eve
       ry
r thing
de grades
grace
       full
full
       to
The
Re
       ader
Thankful
       ly
mus
       ic
es
       mirabilis
do
       me
hurt
       ling
blue
       ceiling

common
         er
red
       deem
           er
mast

a town beyond the seas
but all its streets even endless were
wout gate or wall

Things
       native
sweet
       ly
grow
       Oaths
wr
       earth

a hopeful faithful city
set
a horses ministry feetwards
sky
alluvium at Crowneast (vulg. Crowsnest)
Godshill in the isle of wight (of man)
where the pain of love took all sleep from him
Gadredehope
Salwarpe
Worcester
dane nailed to the door
not one of them forgotten
arrow bow before
Trench lane via Trench Woods
Tan wood to Hill Pool

Ambrosiæ Petræ
this moving stone
men-amber
amber-stone
anointed rocks
Hoar Apel Treo

I have said Ah! to write
inquired up and outward
look for the longwhile
felt for his wounds

red banners blue operas

the brown sea racing
was grassy and plain
wild warm blood mixing

and what of boat
and what of host
and all it coming
from th' jar

The pit sides have fallen in
embers in
my dwelling shook through a person

unstable with lights over
a 1940 Flanders field
a scene unclarified
alone did we return
bulk through the ivory gate
we must not have too great a passion
because &

O because
If the son of man perish
sirs you are set for sorrow
the sea gull is inland
there will be rain
awash one word two ills
pollarded elms   espalierd haw

I know the smallest parts

am lost to the middle

hue

   and through indecipherable

and a over indecipherable

why a stone building

Dirt dirt does cover

pink

 a rose is in its blow

she came—is gone—we have met

because &

O because

skin fell from him as a drape

but I must needs stand firm

he must stir with his hands

gold-friend

in no wise the twisted gold a body

sea-birds bathing

I took my gladness in the cry of the gannet

I put it under foot

breaking into small shares rills & streams

Some of the things is mostly about

Into the orchard shade

tw'n Mars & Averil

and west-wood hill springs new

who writ a discourse of bells

& wheat

these rivers sudden red waters

I have not earned bread

insink to my knees

With earth to take up

The village fiancé

the murderer

having chosen

having been

the victim

stream of minnows

under suffocating cork

light full

ritual a buoyant

death

a patch of sun light

on a carpet weave

nocturnal frame

threads of scarlet, blue

animal choked with bark

Of green or devastating green

malfeasant lawn

Malaison Malaison

wren in season

from above

The deers let out on lawns

cloud closed

in on April

murder rer rers sorrow

wed widowed

snow now naught

Der earth her the

hand led

grace gray beaut

lactal lord out sores

----

day break

ernemorwe

aurora consurgens

dropping honey

in luce

flos campy

transeamus

transeamus

that alone before me

tota pulchra es

a fleur borne in the wound

ded earth wet with

led tears

Let us go on

Each time branching three times growing

Jeal ous days

to rise in mornings

Waylaway

Waylaway

water

golden wristed

Evening Evening

Long tables folded

after the eating

fêted fêted

dress in white windows

ash peach flesh

sleeping sleeping

To blisse lede us that hath noon ende

Waylaway

Waylaway

II. Stranges

Rowing one April

still   wearing   the gloves worn small

a wall one one side

oon two sides

eye glass

in side the breast

when you open them again

Flora

the sails of the herring fleet

so we come back to words

heliotropes

fanciful dead

without

without friendship

the brutes

where your head is

your head

I see your face

under your face

under your arm

then all faces

have only seen one town

must have seen others

from the window

a mash of canals ways

above what the waist rose and fell

a dipper's beak

midway in fury

ore of onion

dandelion

huge hands on the blue

making a lion head

This space where is I mean

tucked without flinch

a rich wine will flood thee

nor torment in fruit

how it does taste

love imbolden us

yea and with insensible creatures

inconsolable wights

The birds sang down

the lover

Dawn

awoke

the birds ended their song

the lover died for his beloved

I drink of your plummage

ile get me up before the Sun

ile cut me boughs off many a tree

pierced by a silver golden flood

a primrose path to cloudless

o plant in me

o seed a plant

Orchards of fruit and Narcissi

Than

to folly

break

crack

It is the fifth of May

in a room built

for sunlight and plants

many years ago

when I cannot be accurate

with the subject at hand

Crack

to folly

than

break

So far

walks the path

makes around

trees proceed

light

Around it is a green flutter

yellow bright on a bronze red

owning a moment to create

not monument nor over

A season of hares & sermons, the rest follows

room will outdoors

drawing apart the stays

So be mused

in mud was I

Yet through a spell of falling

self recognized its mime but still

and turning this other will around

found time in its present little stall

sad goes to garden with all happiness

roots plants in a healthy rot

refusing my hand to take a hand

leaving one standing goes

III. Uninverse

Then and only then

of memory and though

the clarity of the voice at the ford

that had come upon her while she drowsed

a fourth figure

moving as it were

over water

pitched on sorrow

crack and sometimes break

a deep path over the open field

over a stile turned over

the poppy leaves less paper than we thought

turns fleshy grey

The thrushs history

stark radiance today

not free nor destiny

on zeros agony

put not as victory

valour

all pinned out saviour

If you

you would find the hedges white again in may

I name no thing nor I mean no thing

rain air

you mannot see

IV. Night

My self to Christ

in onanist

wasp pierce and pierce in joy

my open tongue

Came! in sound I showed

and sweetness of that song

they may not learn

and joying she sings and singing she longs

as it were a pipe of love

the wasp enters my thigh

heat sweetness and song

This now has been a place I cannot

purge

game

illumi

thigh

music

thigh

rapture of cloth

V. Vestment

for now it is

the Aire is the outward refreshing

where this vast creature breathes

was a Branch planted in

thy Court

a Guest a mole

Heaving the Earth to take Aire

a Roote whose flowres are the Second and Third person

for that water we read

was a second substance

celestial ocean

whose face is beauteous

a Black-bag

amongst visibles

her cupid

Extract a Venus from the sea

The Air is corpus our Animal Oyl

a moyest silent fire

she moves she stands like

wheels in drie

When the child builds a city

Ashes of vegetables

for there shall be no more sea

scorning to attend this piece of clay

plugged mouth of locust

sand Signum for Signatum

He suffers a dream bones

bowl slashed but the sky

bouquets in are turning

VI. A Nation

We were placed were We

too much discuss too much

because we fleur

an operative medium

we wings in yellow

faulty frail

the leaves infusion stains our teeth

a loving Jackal waits

beneath there is of course significance

Yarrow Golden-rod bobs

down in down

pour blue hills under

orange violet

in violent light

cloud conducts to cloud

all dark outloud

Who is it in the Spanish Cape

Who tries to sit upon whose knees

One is barren One aborts the Other hosts a bloody hoard

The tired master imitates

the pupil always is too late

under the Gables under the blue shadows

a bee inquisitive another hanging bee

When will this matter come to matter

When noon comes to roost

somewhere in the sea are sea-lions

different from the land

the reeds in wind

sink my continual

blink me blank me lies away

peering ash—pective

pave me laws away

from all but that blears

all winter lone—aspect

on love love & re last pay

England's my conjure!

England's my conjure

VII. Flight

How many various green
Your pain will lift you

The metal portals grew in Sanctity
The roots bourne downwards in the deep
our sight devoured our sight

our Mansion opened for the passage of its corridors
far flows the stream beyond the mill
a stagnant pond left of the only house
Curtain'd indigo

shaking in your wakefulness choosing cloth to wear
we wish to visit
figures from oure past
to unearth purses lost on walks
to reconstruct the stiles
to upturned fields
one of many fathers works aright
a woman reads to sleep
our figure passing thru a glass distilled
until the child raises itself
a man, a worm repeats its virgin birth
in pink evening his friend under a cloud
blessed with death's nativity ,
a dark hermaphrodite we stood
the thrush and turf spanning the worm
immortal labours of my day

The gate brakes always open
a web reality a mantled pool

Felpham
felpham
felpham

A roller & two harrows lie before my window
Father, The Gate is Open
witnessed by the speculative eyes
Our Garden Guardian Wings
we hear the west howl at a distance

Great Darling Broach
Great Miser Skyward Falling
empty me your pockets
rain fall rain me out
a flooding basket weaves my home

Yellow Dusterer
Yellow Pepperer

Spare me the prospect of my second death
Spare me the prospect of my carpeting

all quitted self
wanders from the source
basking in idle inane

Mark me a savage wasterer
hold me upon my broken cart

laughter has hardly entered
love let to seed
a widowed songerer
hold me a tree top feast

Who fell from intimates
huddled a meagre Cars conveyancy

I am an arm of myself
a fingered pattern
The lightest leafs of Basil

out does its last effort
soil befalls soil
Yellow Plasterer
Barbaric Dusty Drunk

An Ocean Bank, Night
Yellow Blue Whisperer
Still days heat settled in the bottled space
tree to tree, A friend lover washing
Night Blooms, Rare Desart pressed in a thousand leaves
Unseen Waters, Upturned eyes
in the mushroom roots
Green Night, Flowsy
Red Flatterer
Calling backwards at the staring Night

gnarld fruit forct-kiss on the turning floor
where pure could taste the sweets
face to each face the members
grapple held like the bowless
harvest apple

Green Passionates
night laundresses

closed eyes to rid the imbalance

Mister Smithe from Wuster
dies in secret

How many various green
Your pain will lift you

Sonnets of Dubious Authenticity

A Suite of three Stanza Songs
This Set of Nine Songs Signed "Content"

The development of three quatrains each separately
assigned to each of the three persons

When it is a torso
gives to creases
not of obvious breathe
do you decease oblivious

Grace may be infused
tradition and the bridegroom stand aside
light or the bringer of light
shall not confuse the bride

Knocke as behold
held by a voices arm
to breake bold the fathers band
whos hand bends to the son

Three songs

A Cancer Song

My wearied chest commands a broken in
a faithful city washed
please   flood
keep meeting red

of the many sounds never to reach
surrounds our daylight vision
grit, pumice, untread ungrazed
thin as a lamb's ear our having

so ample in its light
I do not bring into
the apple boughs
the amber fruit

Three Stanzas Concerning Aspect of February

feast days that feast on each
addict to our own history
babble towers or sewers
the lesson learning not to teach

this land-like water-colours
this is made of that
the purple-lilac lavenders
the green to blue

raising a red-faced choir of lads and maids
in servitude rejoicing in old songs
for they were never sung before
this way nor ever shall once more

Three Stanzas Concerning The Presence of History in Our Kingdom

The yard empties in August fields
History of a struggle rooms
with shining dust and debris flourishing
our armours edge our embrace

We are defined, recalled, by fruit
imported to this land we rent
being imperial in matter we
decay as mother-daughter to the moment

uncounting countenances of our race
where we place order in the face
of winding unclarity. Father
who we-made as night times day

Two Stanzas Concerning the Physical Nature of Language

Seen after a Bright sky
Light the black writings green
Before I understood this place
All wanted was a garden (scene)

paper linen grass or fruitless weeds
on my own dust mere dust it is
In slow letters of light
A place and no more is set down

ECCO HOME

I have come comfortless down
slown not for you but around
here nothing grows because of love
plants do not for our delight

How can I urn this peace
a fire smoulders through the grain
our teeth, bones, skin, hair
encounters in itself the same

For I am every new dead thing
departed from in moving no more moved
Waters as running keeps never un-begun
wanted desires the up-rooted Son

you move upon the quiet
disquieting rocks
the red blues underneath
our absent's grief

what joys you jars amock
our avenues of trees
whose greening in the winters
bless our disbelief

after this long in
your face I am
the features of my weakening
all that we have made falls in this space

Anon. Lyrics

Eleven Stray Songs and Dialogues Without

A steppin walk most zunny walk
isle of light water there zunny glade show
my dark boat push out from the damp shady stump
done worry my children done worry my chile
so sleek skinned my love is and fresh as the pale
milk morning the morning the make woken stool
dont hide me from that done hide me from this
the gridiron fire the fire dogs digs
you gave me you gave me the money you gave me
my zunny walkover my zunny walk on
my flower mon fleuryon changelion walk
wake in the shady and walk in the zun

This skull is Helen
and you will see
Hyacinth and Narcissus
only bones bare skulls alike

I am walking understone
Soul: I am your naked seat
Body: gravel bed over my head
eaten my heart and my white side

glade us (give us joy)
lull lullay lullaby

Thy face when I may see
my fender of my fose
my salve of my sare
my well my well

now this fools singit
what has you meant

Come into the shepherd aching with God

into the house-field aching with water

come into the orchard armied with sheep

into the green-trees loaded for him

The olive blade sharpen

the straw-latch open

My widow ravished by a new desire

windowed naked as the outside weathers

snow sleet rain upon upon

artichokes, cucumbers, persimmon tree

Sweet mother I
The Candles rimless sea

Lines all longing
eye stands for the hole

's   light
des   pair

ECCE HOMO

where to
get a march on night

servant   to the ordinary
cock or cuckoe crow
hives
all rivers is The World the rivers is
all answers rivers is
her son crossen
(grown to the limit of their crown
(grown huge)
grown huge

O in me there is nought
no debt on doubt
in such surcoat of grey
whereout dropt outward dews
old greycoat on a day
of Amber hair
the gazers eyne
such as a ne'er seen
And fear his weeds and sorrow wear

Calendar Mundi

When I sung to you
at evening
or yesterday
I was apart
from your apparent
burning tuber / on the pile
lets forward with a blue

quick in my eclipsing
low sound I almost
do not hear
so sing
into our dearest house
this moment now

immemorial
touch   glorious

May

From what I do not
come Queen of Moths in company
January a winter's day
As sheep put down a flock
it is along slowly
the path worn more narrow
than a mam up up

the breeze is stop
is not
a hill becomes a shadey dome
a fence of bindweed shallow grown
we weed in may
forward to Hay

try December

when it came to being
so it might
my darling ws sd

want totake some
thing
ws sd

flash of may
be a palace
soft cricket
s gentle whis
p ring field

ws patient

Goody: all creatures looking at my broad windows

patient: after still
        your wrist break

Awoke: after a still price
        Goody chimes into
        go on it is there
        we are loving

now that the gone
the snow-white now no more
to the dead swallow wakes in hollow
tree   the   grass   or   icy   lift
And makes it tender
means we do not say

we has a home

how to go there
at doors   a   country   sweet with   booze
he winds to make

as is already happened is before
all scattered lay did pore upon
what is already done
could want outlook that mark

we   see
we   do
not   know

One seasons
reply
one fields
reply
arrives the lark
the hedge th
rush cuck
oo one seas on

Miscellaneous
Histories

A June Book

All day I lay now in a reverie
the smell of dank and humid grass
try(tried) to climb out (with) terrible
A liquid man is at my elbow
(A liquid man here at my elbow now)

There were these dolls on every surface
And must I sing? What subject shall I choose
Follow a shadow still it moves apace
curious imitation thrills at you

I Why I Write Not [Now] of Love
It is enough conspicuous
Here where I lay at what I have
at home these dolls on all the surfaces

Some act of Love (and some do not)
surprised to find here in their very eye
that what they love (and some do not)
is mere reflection of another's gaze

*

I wrote about the night bird cries
these inmates mingled intimate
days they said were (sounds)(seas) closed.

*

I wrote them with ink in this paper
In Ark, or chest
The great reaching cedars
Child in Sex

*

There was this awful beauty still
        pearl or Dew etc we see
        breast as she passes me
        where can we borrow such
        If once were near enough

    *

The mower's drone
the drone's
so summer high summer
laughters own

    *

In spring across the street
a bright white tree
In April on the stones the leaves

    *

Rose leaves fell on (other)(lower) flowers

    *

Dear Sir
        I have a desk this summer like
        squat like no other
        shit like here I shall be
        (to write) like it were better

    *

Heroes and rogues out of the Hedgerows
pour over us—The Prim-rose pale
in grass—aroused by the thin dark green
some of us by mean stems grow

Some of us wrongs some of us (we doesn't even Know!)
who comes down to here
next neighbours driven out
by the Greenfinch (& Warblers sing)

                    *

Come in Ma'Lord
Down to the Chancey
Come near Ma sweet lord
in to the swim

Drink up Ma song
Heavy and Heaven
Drink me up sweet
Honey and wine

For I have Fetched out
only to love you
Run about wild
all for that juice

                    *

Down in Dark Summer
in the Dank Woodway
in the midge cloudy
I saw a lady

Under green hedges
Undercurled fern leaves
Under white root stock
I saw a Lady

In the still mill pond
Under the algae
Under the wheel stone
Under the weir path
Down in the dock field
Under the tarpaulin
In the soft wood shed
In the bat droppings

Creaking the hinges
Cracking the gatewood
rusting the wheel pins
dusting the shelf

*

Days may coincide with night
Historical I walk within the field
wild date and timelessness upset
as dark fruit pushed out in a place

*

The Entertainments: or, Porch-Verse

Say some sticks in your mind
we have short time to stay
so kind we may together
her young bed I'm sent to
you haste away your hours do

the peacocks that had been attracted
in twos about the lilac trees
behind for these most greedy of all birds
she at once got off her knees

*

They ate the meal prepared a century ago
We disappear—how can we but our time comes on.
as surely as the hunted—eating now
and then one day aware or unaware our time comes on

The myrtle and the herbs must be protected when the frosts
          come on
have called you gathered you to say good night
A little fish a little roasted lamb
and surely as the hour our time comes on

Cake rich as leaf mould dropsy and drugsy
grubs on beetles lice in wooden juice
rock juice grass roots as yarrow cow parsley
This picnic entitled "end of the Summer"

                    *

On Greenwich Hill under the dials
The trees under the heading springs
turning the while to see the isle
of dogs and silver Thames

Barnes Bridge Chiswick King Edward VI
We took to Kew then Richmond Hill
Wild Parrots screaming to us following
a strung up cormorant

I want the garden finished soon
(These house by the river where)
This yellow drawing room
Painters and their Subjects Lived

                    *

Yesterday was the day of miracles
sent straight from the blue sky
I was all day answering it
lying in the fields Glittering Oxon

The Giotto is tiny and pretty
I made my way into the city
I have just read your lovely letter
Agony washed down the figures

*

The birds rising with the aeroplanes
Twenty to two on Shipbourne Common
fruit leaves flick upwards in rain

*

what if you do not speak of truth (the truth)
In this epoch-era when we do not speak of truth
We sexual about in secret
we want to know what root
we are—the goodly rabbit or
the virus but
what was that difference again
rain and then some sun
What if we do not speak of the truth
What if no-one speaks here of the truth

*

The wild hare is up over it
longing to make his hole
'look at that old man—he's nine'
Longing to make the field

*

made space (left alone)
Dreams of all sex
concern in the corners
just what am I building

blues cooeing in the eves
some brown between sheets
my lips were thick and warm and red
her naked in her skirts above my throat
". . . All my hard bones go wild with music notes
here in the rain . . ."
my creamy mouth my tulip head

*

OLOR SEVERNUS

Here on a silent, shady green
And drink all sense and cares away
Whether the sun had been King
or waking (the banks) their discontent
Day her face now meant
no accident or sight (now) absent
makes a tie of influence
out senses us nor west nor east create
Here and Here and How it is is meet

*

Leverett and eel-black
by tangled
stillwater
grubs. Baring my
branches and twigs
peeling antler

*

Hop-trellis'd Hill
green canopy reminded
dairies orchard goose
loose copse gorse ferns
up to the broad lazy-path
Malverns, Worcester beacon
British Camp cut rugged furrows
Ironage defences, barrows
tumuli-overlook of School & Priory
and further, Pershore-abbey
bridge-ridge of Woodbury
Bredon, Evesham Valley
and through it gracefully
the Avon and the Severn
Teme and Salwarpe lead
here Will, I sit
away from now till
a further day.

*

dilapidated Morris, green rover
hymn singer on blue bicycle
the scent of fifty or more elderberry
over ford, yarrow Queen Anne's lace
bees flies on excrement

*

To be off the ground
To look out a little farther
The taste of Water

*

All night by [the] rose, rose
All night by the rose I lay
Trip a little with the foot
And let The body go

*

How do you lay down on the apple now
Why do you sleep so on the apples knee

A man is died for us to live upon
        How do you . . .

Take all you own and sell it to your son
        How do you . . .

I cannot go til you will come again
        How do you . . .

A narrow view with all the field to roam
        How do you . . .

A sparrow in and out the radiant Hall
        How do you . . .

The blood is in those feet so far away
        How do you . . .

*

What fish in what dark night catches the net
I must admit I sink into whateverness without
the eyes rolled over and my foes and fingers swollen in my mind
to child proportions—teeth bite on Chalk(sponge) like porpoises
And all I thought I wanted was to sleep awake but
day and night have never meant me yet

curlewing fancy in the scrappy copse
whirling our heads over our heads
we have come out tonight into the grazing field
blind by unstirring night-beasts
(hysterical) then chattering this more than wanting this
clothed in a pocket of our huddle-self

I know that you grow old That I grow old
I do not know such things
Intent on water focusing on focusing
this makes and then this makes
only to realize the endlessness of
will you tell me what I said

*

I know I edge towards grief
and when you go I shall be all of it

*

Nothing will move this
is a Holy picture
two figures barely
moving together

entitled <u>Chronicle</u> with "Plot"

709   Hard Winter
710   Hard year and deficient crops
711
722   Great crops
723

756   Plot
757

758   "It is finished" attempt to write beginning middle end
      and to form narrative
760
761   Killing time
762   mostly

Catalogue
Catafalque
more Catalogue

Abstract, the part below the water confines side; Abyss, the lower part.

Adam or Adham, the divided or created part, man home or homo

Babel of Chaldes, the spring water place part, habitation or dwelling place

Brittain, Beritan, Bretan or Bredan inclosing a name given to this island

as a specimen Corn, on the inclosures; obliged to defend the inclosing spring water

Could or Should, at surrounding spring water place. Couple; Courage

Hence Dam or Dame. Damage. Droitwich the surrounding part side or street

Hence Drop; Drought, the surrounding part shut. Drown. England

in the time of the Heptarchy, the water enclosing, Angles or Isle Land

covered by water. End, The inclosing side; Endless, the place below.

Flaw and Flow

Flay the spring place of growth

Gangway or Geld

Hard, the high water side

The I signifying here

no more than the article

Joke, Journey, Joy, the circle of Sun

Iron, the fire one

Keeps, Yorks, the inclosing water side

Leg, the spring place and Legacy at the water place

Letter, on the water place side

Marches or Marshes

Martyr or the faint-like L

Natan-Leod the inclosing water of sea side places, people

or tribes, or the British possessions

along the sea coasts from Hants to the Severn Sea

Hence Obey; Oblige; Oblivion, a flood on the circle part
ON, NO, OR, and Heliopolis
Hence Place; Play or Pleas, the water place side where
Plight and Rain, Hence Reach, the river confines;
Read, the river or flowing divisions or parts
Saint, on the lower sea side
or the cell; Sail on the sea
Tell, above or beyond the covering place, the high light
covering or the sky. Thee, the or side I or man. To
Vow, the surrounding spring oath or woe;
Vowel; Voyage or water edge or action upwards
Weeds, the spring parts; Week or Weak;
Ween, in us. Weep, without spring. Year; the spring on

THE
Garden.
A Theophany

or

ECCOHOME
A Dialectical Lyric

A Mask Beginning:
Enter Chorus (Who is M) Singing:
[Early Asking of the Sun]

Blind Yellow
Where do we follow
has ever answered fully
we slowly inwardly with thy face
Hunting the Green Lion
Whose story pens us

Lyrics from the latifundium
Individual members of the Chorus:

You touch with dead cells touch dead cells
I had been happy in the tent
Waiting on the Summer rain to cease
The Play Between The Acts

I had been happy curled beneath the seat
You touch sweet borders & farewell
Waiting on the drum ear piercing drum
The Play to be content

A leaf shadows across my arm
it is all my movement
A colour worries my eye
my eye it is—these two
split as I am, monster
Your eyes are in a heavy light

Drought and Drowsy with wet
Words Fool & Actors
hang'd an anchor under
air where water wants

---

criminall'd wi'sin
I was will be
even sitting I
It is impossible to begin

As it all it wanted was a stone
dripping with blood and semen
his hair the colour of paper
his hair the colour of straw

Mouth: Are you still?
Still: Still moaning I

That murmurs mumble
tittle tattle is all myself

Call: Call it falling
Not that
Again: Not that
Again: this will or was
The past neither undoes nor does
this I can see
Thankful a cloud replaces one
Joy is it at the mud unsteady muddy
river's edge or our edge

there is despair
a yellow sickness on our surfaces
Yet we shall not survive to vengeance
or authentic anguish
it is over
us in saying naught do not
our surface wrinkles but it is no depth
this moment to the next is not our death
Notice that I
am dead

Ferns, Death & Blessing

I sit without the whole morning
and in the evening we sail about
the sea is all coming down
Donot say this melancholy song
I write nothing but by fits
I am one of the Nobodies
I write little now

an English-made
saw was thus shut out
two huts
with out our knowing who
I would still like to give thanks
[*deletion*] I had written when
withdrawn

Garden

I was a garden planted with beauty
these palaces of self
annihilation
lifting the sun that blinds me
from a soft and mossy universe
The Moon & Lamb
On entering it murders every living thing
or I am murdered
to be in your wholly
& I am its own other then undone
Its beauty O that I could cease to be

A cloud of blood burst in it dazling
forth a salt taste to the elements
and earth it tasted, sun, wind, and
rain came down with it of it in it
Light waves particles it is that
which greens the plant

M: and in the last speeches of M and in the middle act
            he accepted death
He: he dismissed life with grace
M: I have tried to sleep away my time
            and pass two thirds of twenty four in bed
            I may speak of myself as dead
            found hanging on some Oak
He: But when it is all over
            can return to his wandering
            can rhyume hisself with death undead
M: Doom eager runs his story
            there may I give sweet rest
            under some nightloved cedar
He: in day they are our source of night

M: Stay moment and murmur in vain
        it is the light to surfaces that gleam
I dreamt a death
I looked on all the works my hands had wrought
and all was vanity and wreath
He: It was enough to hear
M: It was better never said

I: more idiocy
His words demanded me
M: and more
He: will it never be unsaid
I touch but the things will not come near me
Says a third
M: Our Lover's Anhedonia
witness our world
I: In panic still I run my furrow straight
He: You notice with two laundered shirts
one collar frayed one arm pit stained
and as the evening greys you cannot hope
to stay
M: Burst and decay
I will
remains

The Garden
M: have come here to be found

ECCO HOME

Across from you
the other
side
the gully
rill dell where sound
backs partial repeat

again the discomfort
climb
the paved terraces
that inward portico the under
balconies the shelf pavans
including self Across
valley of south
Sun or on water
fire it went from
East under
trees Man himself
shrank its name
Across
A Natural History of Self:

        his autobiography written in the third person
              as Suso in tender pity
        put a thorn in my nest to prevent me from it
              Shall you become beautiful
        here swarm the worms of sense and re-sent-ment
              O G...the Self...of a think-er...who knows
        who knows I undoes whee needs
              this pipling formality this shuffle
              excuse succumbs
        outside of him this voice and the echo
              must I accompany all our objects
        our antecedent tunnel at the end of our tunnel

Deaths & Blissie

From Deaths: Noone is there
        was there

but Bless you divine
you upturn to fineness
her upraised must
we sweet and buckle
his outworn frown
touching on matters of matter
and learns her gone
and from her leans
and from her goes

It is the body
makes us sad
and mind
and grief

You go travelling disease
pleased by the leaving glow
lifted as a paper errant
in some garden ~~waste~~. Slough

Bliss passes you when all is wash
and lost scavenges the beachy scrap

Call me obscene

we do not sing eternally
we sing eternally

Calling from Blissie then:
            Aflicker was the body lies
            besides the table laden was
            a pair of richly dressed
            particularly emphasized

In one, for instance lovers are
caressing one and one besides
a table richly dressed
with food for instance lovers are

And Bliss addresses them
as follows four for instance
static scenes two pair of lovers were
addressed each other there

If Bliss would make a step to dance
caressing one another here besides
a table laden richly dressed
each other for instance

the image of a Pier eaten sweetly
                        away   a God at every gate
My world bleached to green
to red punctures
my impressions of movement
                        a late catching train
position in this
bark-rough, magnesium hued—leaves which offer various
        edges
As a garden is school, shop sexual encounter
as shoes that will need cleaning
tools returned or borrowed from a place
takes its position in payment
debt, and its inhabitants defined
then a park is the same as myself
is both this other and that

You make choices where to live
but this is not so
an unnamed thing is named
If I am capable of dressing I am dressed
I cannot undress thee

Event   its presence is presented
there must be things at growth
underneath stones in wet abysses
substances sustained—
ing recording silences between
the yawn named in the garden
As Graphael announced—
it is the record of its having been

the garden poems and there's music &
some very strange
I have included nothing but in boundaries

All flesh is grass
and flesh made words
and these you visit as you might a garden seek
sought when the breath blows upon it
surely the people is

I have written that which never was
to that which never is
The planting of this seed annihilates this seed

M: My darling notword planted in the sound
   nutweed knotweeds
   Heroic alphabet—terrible of ants
   My endless mying mind
V(who is M): Voice through the void
            The fifth—element, sonata?
            The fisses in the flod
            all rain above
            memory of love is love
            and death
M: tremble of weeds
   have not heard you
Y(who is M): Is not Jerusalem described
            the goat, the ewe
            nurtured and ground beneath the Yew
M: Ma honey terrible my lonely honey drip
   made by to be the being bees

The text is not secret
Part two
all manner of nones
your objects float before you
choice is jested and irrelevant
this being told this
telling disappointment outweighs delight
for the object weights to subject you
do you suffer to meet

Myself of Song

One here regions or death regions
its lips are dead, its hands hang down
lie like the rotten pool
foulest of smells but for my love
many waters cannot
and the same things will be restored without end

Will: Dear So
    and so
    Sleeping I lead
    with his wife Kit
    made of land
    this little spot of earth
S: The locale where M must choose
  which of the others he will
  picture a dreamer
  plot of green grass
  running water
  The places of their beginnings
  and the songs of birds
  the human head "very pale and discoloured"
  big life in the desart
  big living availed
  there are more crimes than love
  in the Salt white river bed
  over all over a trembling wings
  this to be read
  Dark burning as when
  M's Friend sings M's own song
  back to him
  that is yours
  this carcass's cause
M: make a list of how many how much

M: No   more
I am desperate
la carne gloriosa e santa

We wreck it for we love it so
to stop one moment I am desperate

Break for a little space my song.

High abstracts my meat and bones

When gardens wood has everything
Vanished to the monastery of time
I come off in your looking
(*And even he, towards the end, was encouraged to remember that
he liked asparagus; our lord the Spirit is reluctant to allow either
of the two great Ways to flourish without some courtesy to the
other*)

THE GARDEN:
If I was dying (which we were)
What would I planted here
Asparagus and Thyme for I must learn
to read these two in their seasons
> *Retired from his Military Victory the general becomes the
> corporal*
March in turns comes on
a dark soil in the raised beds does
and I have limed the cold frames
for the cucumbers
but that was years ago
> *compromise does not yet exist as a virtue*
(we mistook Charity for fear of blood
and we still shudder at such blood but
it is fear turned to ecstasy again it is
we have bypassed charity)

Do I have fish in my Garden
A swan
Geese
Yes and a history of assignations in the Orangery
a draught of notes passed
a summer fumed with perchance
Winter heat with future

Who has died in my Garden
Carried off to the island
with this or that ceremony
We have all and will

Are there monuments
to histories, victories
perennial fashions
perhaps

Not that we are not all
have you seen dying, loving
anything any something
who inhabits we are all collected there

My Address needless to say
by a poem we cannot be saved
by your time we are no longer (t)here
More last words
cannot resist this living

It is weather in my Garden
Sun—the first ever Sun
and torrential rain
and dust beading to dirt
I am so Happy I could
leavedrift
hungry I could drink
A young woman
man running water
Johannes *de Silentio*: We know it, all of us—
        it was only a trial

Faced with this lover
but with genitals removed
now hanging from the mouth
This trophy of annihilation

the act to reinvest divestment
It is Abraham's Faith
It is Isaac's Despair
My Address needless to say

You have faith in my Garden for it must exist

For all she saw was
a veil, finer, lighter and yet more concealing
it was an unseen influence
is he to remain silent since
it, too, is also the result of the free acts of the individuals
(*Queen Elizabeth is said, ni fallor, to have been informed of this
and sat ten days with one finger in her mouth, biting it without
saying a word, and then she died*).

QE (who is M): To days of Glossary
not Glossolalia
(*it goes without saying that at the moment of consummation the
tragic hero, like anyone else, is capable of a few words, even a
few appropriate words. But the question is whether it is
appropriate for him to say them*).
He hears his death-sentence
and if we are done
we are done for

EPILOGUE: ECCO HOME

For we are all done
and each generation
begins the human
again and is done
from where it began

Chorus (which is M)
        While I live my pleasant song
        Raise again the joyful sound

Song
>
> Dark Solum That is
> all my mirth & play
> At-a-spring well
> And exiled from
> Darken and Lighten Sweet Solum

Chorus (which is M)
>
> we must learn to be content
> here-in-our mea-ning-less sentence

The Garden : begins and is
The Fire etc
>
> The semblance of speech may be enough:
> I saw him with flesh
> I saw him with blood
> I saw that he brought
> I saw the world of him.

garden a theophany
garment of divinty
whoever this we
all must travel

aleegory: the vehicle completely
        disappears
symbol: tenor must bull on

lover: my myriad wives abandoned in your manyness
self: Liquid'd desire desired

lover: manmade lake ha ha'd for natural subtlety
Self: posting (history)

THE END
as a start perhaps
perhaps a much better
finish or call it ending
let it be known forthwith
as ending

a lilly with five leaves
why not a lily with four leaves?
strange fascinating the great revolving sky
dense air or night-cloud filled

where can I take you
down how few times to the soil
or asleep at the side of it
insect-close I have forgotten

I baptise my Garden the new day
I dive from the hill fort into its roaring lake
all about are horses, the retired symbols
all about are flowers uncut for this age

Quatrain of Earth Trimeter of Heaven
Down to a plain of cedars
In to a dell of elms

(If you are to ask me what discretion you should exercise
in this work, my answer is None whatever!)

For he experiences true sorrow
who knows and feels not only
what he is, but that he is.

fatal chriticism
flowers up the pole
when I have said that what have I done

In this light your hair is almost
white is almost gone is golden

You replace yourself
in our garden spinning as it is
a green is in

We pass under an arch of laburnum it is late afternoon it is
evening the wysteria it is morning we pass over a narrow flint
encrusted bridge late morning we have risen late the daff
profusion it is luncheon early afternoon I am alone we walk along
the dwarf box hedge a meadow planted some but mostly wild
you wait its dark the rain upon the canopy we play bright games

The voice a water garden
as the sound of like a
noise of (of their wings)
of many waters a voice over waters

the rooted and issuing stream
so often at our border

Questions regarding voice and water
            who spoke water
            the lake is no answer
V: In finite words
W: issuing from before the rivers source
V: Tell us those that saw us
W: At first our reflections were mere water

Lake: Like a noise of many voices
          other
Line: linen as text and textile
linnet a songbird feeds on flax
Know, whoever asks my name
that I am Line and go
through a meadow flower-gathering
To Be: The Bee who gathers beauty from the flowers
          other

Further furthest East
I see a Rose
as in a garden closed
But moves Sun rise
the growers mow
in bed
          and rising without
a scent to one outside the gate

Dialogue between Lost & Found
F: Where have we come
L: to lose ourselves
F: In place
L: of selves we have
F: at least
L: at most it is no quantity
F: have you come to the garden
L: What does your fence imply
          which way swings your gate
F: Both ways from its post
L: a post which pins itself to nought
F: how can it
L: yet it does

Dialogue between Garden and Field
Dialogue between Fence and Gate
F: Your freedom is apocryphal
G: Your selvage that which isn't you
F: I can be sat and climbed
G: I can be ridden through
Dialogue between Self
S: Why have you come here
to be found & lost
the Garden is a source
into which nothing can descend
The Gardens same need not repeat
its growing is its end

S: Had you ever thought a Garden might be blind
I never did such colours and for what
S: For sight
a blindman's night
a singer deaf supinely in the green
Where she is single solitary lone
Will no one tell me what she sings
and is she beautiful the cheek that turns away
is she deformed she is as beautiful as you can see
or say

Dialogue between two lovers met in the garden
L: We build a house of You
a wall of face
L: Lamentable of Late
when you are gone I am
We never cosummate our
consummation. Date
eytched on the green bow rings
deformed in anniversary of place

We invent a speaker for these words:

having come already from the greatest distance our speaker appears at the very edge of the Garden I will not say day or night but I may be correct in assuming that a flood has taken place so that the heads of tulips float neck-broken mouths agape and below them their stems yellow into darkness at first our first reckoning of the speaker is a dark reflection a presence in the maze of reflected branches at first we are startled to realize that all this time we have been staring at an image on water not knowing what it really meant

The Epistle of nothing and the shadow
The Epistle of the opened and the closed gate
The Argument to the path and the Stream
The marriage of doing and undoing
The Art of Nothing
Noting

Together we have walked out
into a field
meaning flowers

The experience at stake in the idyll is thus the breaking apart of a habit the rupturing of a habitual dwelling into a surprise The Garden named is the death of The Garden The Garden we inhabit must continually seek to precede and antecede our naming It will do this leisurely We feign thoughts in a habit of naming Our acceptance has not killed The Garden our habit kills us in The Garden which is The Garden in us At the pools edge the reflection must be experienced as the ever other Its name is changing Its name is nothing It lives

If a leaf float out into the reflection
boat into the trees tied to a mirrored post
the bird note attempts

Reflections on a Garden Scene
Made mostly in the rain
From inside
The Garden seems contain
Windowed as it were
the perfect green

*In the midst of all the place was a fair pond whose shaking crystal
was a perfect mirror to all the other beauties, so that it bare show
of two gardens; one in deed, the other in shadows.*

A Song of Blood
this funerary song sans lyre
to our right the tragedians dress
to replace and be replaced by the undressed commedians
A Masque
". . . makes a remarkable contribution."
who lies beyond my tongue I utter such things

In the words of the Chorus
            A robin after rain
            A single robin
            rain
(How can I yet I do)

The Dialogue as Silence
M: The word wants to grasp the voice
W: The Garden is (said that Garden is) dead
V: In you my voice lives. This is the Garden
The Garden is now returned to itself

Return to the Garden : ECCO HOME

Just as it ends
begins in silence
the man sing Daimon
dividing Home divine

The ground under the ground
over the ground digging
In solitude I read
Silence the spade engraved

After my death I listen
The last thing you read has been written

The backside of the house was neither field, garden, nor orchard,
or rather it was both field, garden and orchard; for as soon as the
descending of the stairs had delivered them down, they came into
a place cunningly set with trees of the most taste-pleasing fruits;
but scarcely had they taken that into their consideration but that
they were suddenly stept into a delicate green; of each side of the
green a thicket, and behind the thicket again new beds of flowers,
which, being under the trees, the trees were to them a pavilion
and they to the trees a mosaical floor, so that it seemed that Art
therein would needs be delightfully counterfeiting his enemy
Error and making order in confusion.

Drawings of the Garden
exist. verso an English reverdie
a kitchen garden inventory
Noted three trees quince
Nine of apple (2P, 3C, 4? not sure)
Tree of ornamental Pear (being provided as the emblem of the
        county)
Down thru rows of

Beetroot, Swede, Collards, Endive
Celeriac, Chokes, Aubergine.
verso drawings number I-IX
The Garden prospective
a system of canals, cuniculi
a viaduct off chasms precipice
a system of tiered lagoons
resevoirs for trout and carp
a trolley pumped fanicular
brass weighted gates a pulley
latch released a dial an armillary sphere a speculum
front elevation
rear prior to orangery
this name "the vines" vinea? vinetum?
various hortulus (cucumber, asparagus)
a templum for birds

There were hills which garnished their proud heights with stately trees; humble valleys whose base estate seemed confronted with refreshing of silver rivers; meadows enamelled with all sorts of eye-pleasing flowers; thickets, which, being lined with most pleasant shade, were witnessed so to by the cheerful deposition of many well-tuned birds; each pasture stored with sheep feeding with sober security, while the pretty lambs with bleating oratory craved the dams' comfort; here a shepherd's boy piping as though he should never be old; there a young shepherdess knitting and withal singing, and it seemed that her voice comforted her hands to work and her hands kept time to her voice's music. As for the houses of the country—for many houses came under their eye—they were all scattered, no two being one by the other, and yet not so far off that it barred mutual succour: a show, as it were, of an accompanable solitariness and a civil wildness.

B's cottage at Felpham
emanation over the hand pump
God or Angel in the Garden
Lo you are here now

Chorus
      singing (signing) Being's oblivion
      It goes without saying
      Beauty what are you doing today

Yesterday I sat in a place
that sounds incredible

The morning of
Indeed the afternon
The first scene discovers a wilde wood
attendant Spirit descends or enters
the homestead giddy giddily
while ill I'll lie the island in its yellow grey
your health in being
green it cannot be

Enter Heaven and GoldenAge
      House & Garden
      Hearth & Gate
      Here & Gone
H: when builded here

G: before these buildings were

H: remember if you can

G: the child beneath the man

H: these out buildings in use

G: of the original house